Barbara Belding
Zanzibar Dec. 2002

ZANZIBAR STYLE

Published in 2001 by The Gallery Publications
P.O. Box 3181, 170 Gizenga Street, Zanzibar
e mail: gallery@swahilicoast.com
www.swahilicoast.com & www.galleryzanzibar.com

London office:
32 Deanscroft Avenue
London NW9 8EN
e mail: zjafferji@aol.com

ISBN 9987 667 01 5

© 2001 The Gallery Publications
Photographs by © Javed Jafferji
Written by © Gemma Pitcher
Designed by The Swahili Coast Publishers
Printed in Singapore

All pictures are available for commercial use from:
Javed Jafferji: javed@swahilicoast.com or
Impact Photos: library@impactphotos.demon.co.uk
Gemma Pitcher is available for assignments: gemmapitcher@hotmail.com

All rights reserved. No part of this publication may be reproduced, stored in a retrieval system or transmitted, in any form or by any means, electronic, mechanical, photocopying, recording or otherwise, without the prior written permission of the publishers and the copyright holders

DEDICATED TO HASIBA & ABBAS

ZANZIBAR STYLE

JAVED JAFFERJI • GEMMA PITCHER

THE GALLERY PUBLICATIONS
ZANZIBAR

CONTENTS

Introduction	17
Swahili Style	20
Details • Textiles	40
Details • Barazas	44
Details • Tingatinga	48
Details • Games	52
Indian Style	56
Sultans' Style	78
Details • Doors	108
Colonial Style	112
Land & Sea Style	134
Details • Spices	172

Left: Bungalow, Chumbe Island Coral Park.
Following page: *Baraza* space, Sultan Palace hotel.

Above: *Dema* - traditional fish trap.
Right: Colourful *Mkeka* mat.
Following page: Misali island, Pemba.

Left: Lobby, Tembo House Hotel, Stone Town.
Above: Four poster, Serenity apartment, Stone Town.
Following page: Breakfast room, Chumbe Island Coral Park.

INTRODUCTION

"In Zanzibar", David Livingstone once remarked, "Nothing is quite as it seems". And Zanzibar is indisputably a place of contradictions. The high, white townhouses, mosaic-lined fountains, honey-skinned women in long black veils - this could be Marrakesh or Algiers. Brightly coloured cotton, wound around ladies making their stately way home from market, baskets of flour balanced on their heads - are we perhaps somewhere in the great hot interior of Africa? Latticed balconies, Hindu films on show at the cinema, sari silks, scented with sandalwood, on sale in the market - surely India? While on the jetty, chaps in splendidly crumpled white suits and ladies in cool linen take an evening gin and tonic as the sun goes down and discuss the latest gossip from -Surrey? or Sandton?

Puzzling as it may be to visitors, Zanzibar's residents don't seem to regard their island as an enigma, or see anything strange in their mix of cultures. Ever since the first sailors stumbled onto its shore in search of fresh water and sustenance, Zanzibar has been assimilating new ways of building, decorating, speaking and dressing. To and fro across the Indian Ocean went merchants, princes, buccaneers and pirates, plying back and forth between Persia, Oman, Portugal, Britain or the African interior. Every new arrival who disembarked from a merchant cutter or an Arab dhow brought something new to add to the landscape of Zanzibar - a beaten gold pot, a bolt of bright cloth, an ivory tusk or a clove tree seedling.

As a result, living in Zanzibar involves getting to know not just one culture, but several, all so closely intertwined that the joins between them are almost invisible. Little piles of translucent noodles are arranged symmetrically on the stalls of street vendors alongside roasted cassava roots. Africa and China, meeting on a trade wind, exchanged recipes. Out in the shamba - the countryside - men sip cups of black Arabic coffee under the mango trees. They're wearing long, white robes and tiny embroidered caps, but their faces are African.

The visitors who came ashore from ships carrying spices from India, slaves from the African interior, or bolts of cotton from America, decided to stay, and introduce a few home comforts while they were about it. The Swahili who were there already had a few of their own ideas to pass on, too.

Left: Staircase, Emerson and Green hotel.

And slowly the great melting pot of Indian Ocean culture simmered into spicy, vibrant life.

Zanzibar style is about the coming together of living traditions from all the so-called dhow countries - those nations who once traded silks, slaves, ivory and spices by making use of the monsoon winds to blow them in their wooden vessels across the Indian Ocean. It is also about the traditions of mainland Africa, brought to Zanzibar by slaves and slave-takers from the shores of the great lakes. Finally came the colonialists, bringing with them the pompous grandeur and 1930's chic of the hunting safari, the tea dance, the tennis match.

These days the boundaries have become blurred, and Zanzibar has an instantly recognisable style of its own. You'd be hard put to find a room in any Zanzibari house in which traditionally Arab, Swahili, Indian and western objects don't sit side by side in perfect harmony, each with its own place in the decorative scheme.

In the tall, narrow houses of Stone Town, the rooms furthest from the street are darkest and quietest, with small windows and thick wooden shutters which, when opened, allow the occupants to reach out and touch the wall of the house opposite. For sunlight and a view, one climbs a storey higher to the tea house on the rooftop, to sit among scattered cushions on the floor, watching the sails of dhows bobbing in the harbour.

Beds are four poster and elevated so high off the ground that a footstool is needed to step into them. The frames are carved in rosewood with glass covered panels at the head and feet, depicting fruit and flowers in bright, earthy reds and blues. Mosquito nets hang four-square from the frames above. Niches are everywhere, cut into stone walls or let into the front of dressing tables. Each contains something - a little porcelain vase full of artificial flowers, a beaten bronze lamp, a makonde spirit carving in ebony, or simply the TV remote control.

A sudden eruption of voices from somewhere outside in the street, an argument or child's tantrum, is a reminder that there is a whole world of noise and hustle just outside the old wooden shutters. At night, cats yowl and slide up and down the corrugated iron roofs outside. Sometimes, at dusk, bushbabies come out from the tree outside and utter piercing shrieks under the windowsills, wanting the bananas that are left out to feed them. In the mornings, tinny Taarab music rises up from the alleyway below, together with the smell of coffee brewing and the limpid, bubbling sound of Swahili mothers hurrying their children to school. Five times a day the air is split by an amplified muezzin's wail from the mosque across the street, joined in chorus a few seconds later by the others, dotted around the old quarter and beyond.

By the sea, on the shimmering beaches of the coast, or in the dense, green plantations of the interior, the textures are rougher and the etiquette of living more relaxed, with everyone thrown together at closer quarters. Sand is everywhere, patiently swept out every morning by ladies with their cotton khanga pulled up comfortably between their knees. Inside, brightly coloured makuti mats describe concentric circles on the floor. The furniture consists of string and wood beds, stick chairs, and rough wooden tables holding piles of shells collected from the beach. Fish traps made of split bamboo serve as lampshades. Vibrant cotton cushions line the walls.

The doors in a Zanzibari village are never shut - to enter, one simply stands outside and shouts "hodi" (may I enter?) until someone replies "karibu!" (welcome!). Neighbours spend as much time in each others' houses as their own, the women plaiting hair or peeling garlic together in companionable silence. The men gather together under palm-thatch shelters, playing bao or cards or discussing the buying and selling of land. Children concentrate on recycling rubbish into new toys - racing cars painstakingly assembled from strips of metal cut from tins, or sunglasses made from strips of bamboo poles or banana leaves.

The idea of a communal meeting place is deeply ingrained in Zanzibari culture, based around the Islamic practice of gathering in the mosque for prayers several times a day. People gather together whenever they can - on street corners, on the baraza benches outside their houses, and around the men who sell coconuts from baskets on the back of bicycles or coffee from brass pots set on top of charcoal braziers.

To live in Zanzibar, then, one must leave behind the pressures and priorities of the Western world, and tap in instead to a pace of life which simply waits to see what turns up on the next boat. One must forget the tiny, individual boxes into which much of the world divides up its inhabitants; and grow used to a life where everything is shared - living space, meals, quiet moments in the heat of a long afternoon. One must learn to grow closer to one's neighbours by exchanging a series of courtesies until the boundaries between private and public space become blurred and family and friends have no distinction. And most important of all, one must learn from the Zanzibaris themselves the customs of tolerance and hospitality, of relaxed and easy conversation, simple, cool living spaces and slow-burning friendships.

Right: Private apartment, Shangani, Stone Town.

introduction 19

SWAHILI STYLE

I longed to travel about the world and visit distant cities and islands in quest of profit and adventure. So I bought a great quantity of goods, made preparations for a new voyage, and sailed down the river Tigris to Basra. There I joined a band of merchants and set sail the same day. Helped by a favourable wind, we voyaged for many days from port to port and island to island; and wherever we cast anchor we sold and bartered our goods, and haggled with officials and merchants. At last our ship reached the shores of an island, rich in fruit and flowers, and echoing with the singing of birds and the murmur of crystal streams.

The Second Voyage of Sindbad the Sailor
Tales from the Arabian Nights

While most of Europe was still floundering in what we now call the Dark Ages, the light of the Oriental world had already fallen on Zanzibar. It nestled in the middle of a well-established mercantile civilisation, constructed from a series of independent coastal and island city-states, which stretched down the East African littoral from the Somali coast to the mouth of the Zambezi river.

The Swahili civilisation was born on the coast of Africa, and nourished by the waters of the Indian Ocean, criss-crossed for centuries by merchant vessels bearing traders and adventurers - or pirates - from India, Arabia, Persia, China, Japan and even Russia. They arrived on the East African coast with the north-east monsoon, and left again, their holds groaning with trade goods, on the *kusi*, the south-west wind. They brought metal tools, weapons and jewellery, and took away ivory, tortoiseshell, slaves and palm oil. The 9th century *Tales of Sindbad the Sailor* from the eastern fairytale of the Arabian Nights reflect the seafaring tradition of the peoples of the Persian Gulf. It was they who named the coast *Zanj el Barr*, meaning 'land of the black people'.

The African people of the coast intermarried with the visitors, fusing their traditions with Arab customs until the Swahili became a distinct race - named from the Arabic word *Sahil*, meaning coast - with its own language, feudal rulers, art forms and decorative traditions. Driven from their homes by a succession of wars and conflicts that beset the countries of the Persian

---

Left: This *ngalawa* outrigger canoe, of a type used for centuries by Swahili fishermen, today provides a hiding place for children on Kizimkazi beach.

Gulf at intervals. Shirazi and Arab visitors settled permanently in Swahili towns, bringing the new religion of Islam with them.

The Swahili had no one overall ruler - they were organised into separate communities, each ruled by its own sultan, but with a constant flow of populations between the trading centres that rose and fell with the progression of the centuries. Zanzibar was ruled by a dynasty of kings and queens, with the hereditary title of Mwinyi Mkuu. The Mwinyi Mkuu were Islamic rulers, but credited with older powers - they held in their possession a set of magic drums, which beat of their own accord when the kingdom was in peril. The last Mwinyi Mkuu died in 1873, and his mansion at Dunga in the centre of Zanzibar island is thought to be haunted.

Zanzibar rose to prominence as a flourishing commercial centre in the thirteenth century. Swahili communities on Zanzibar and Pemba built stone mosques decorated with carved inscriptions, minted silver coins and used delicate Syrian-style perfume bottles in green and blue glass. The graves of their more important citizens featured stone towers at either end, with Chinese porcelain bowls sunk into the cement walls. Mosques and private dwellings had dressed stone lintels, rectangular, patterned wall-niches, plasterwork friezes and stone latticed windows. The Swahili decorative tradition arose from the fact that the dictates of Islam forbade the rendering of images of people or animals. Patterns on walls, ceilings, furniture and utensils were always abstract, or composed of verses from the Koran in Arabic lettering. The floors of the richer houses were covered with Persian rugs. Wealthy women went about richly decorated with gold and silver jewellery, and prosperous merchants wore robes and turbans embroidered with gold thread.

Swahili houses - few examples of which remain on Zanzibar - were built of fossilised coral 'rag' held together with limestone cement and thatched with makuti palm leaves. Stone benches ran around the outside porch, providing a space known as a *daka* where the master of the household received visitors. A carved, double-leafed wooden door led into the interior of the house. The privacy of the women of a Swahili household was jealously guarded, their quarters being in the innermost recesses of the house beyond an inner courtyard, and visited only by the closest family members. In the wealthier areas of Swahili towns, covered walkways crossed high above the streets to allow well-born women to glide between houses without being seen by the eyes of strangers.

Swahili domestic furniture - many examples of which remain on Zanzibar today - was both decorative and ingeniously designed. Food trays had saucers to hold dishes at either side, corn grinders incorporated large flat stones, and high-backed, formal wedding chairs were inlaid with ivory or bone. Babies' cradles woven from cotton cloth hung from the ceiling or from struts of springy wood. Beds were wooden frames, often carved, covered with coir rope made from coconut husks. They were sat on during the day, slept on at night, and carried the dead to their graves. Brass coffeepots, trays and lamps were decorated by hammering or chiselling.

But above all, the Swahili were a seafaring people. Their boats were sewn, or held together with wooden pegs, and the prows were carved into the likeness of a camel's head and hung with banners of cloth and talismans to keep them from sinking. The building of ships was a highly-skilled craft practised by itinerant master shipbuilders. They would go into the woods themselves to pick out the timbers, which were then fumigated with incense while the blessings of Allah were invoked. Once built, the launch of a ship was a festive occasion attended by the whole community, at which chapters from the Koran were read.

As early as the first century AD, Zanzibar was mentioned in the account of a Greek sea-captain as being famous for the wicker baskets in which the inhabitants caught fish. Fish traps are still seen in modern Zanzibar, fashioned from split bamboo or palm ribs and pentagonal in shape. Traditional vessels - outrigger canoes, carved from the trunks of mango trees, *ngalawa* with exotic curved sails and cargo-carrying *jahazi* drift across the harbour between modern-day container ships and luxury yachts.

In Zanzibar today, Swahili artefacts decorate hotel lobbies and private houses, and men still weave through the crowded streets of Stone Town wearing long, flowing white *kanzu* (robes) and embroidered *kofia* (hats). Swahili cuisine - curries made with coconut milk and spices, *maandazi* pancakes, fried octopus - is eaten daily by most of the population, and the traditional music of the Swahili coast, Taarab, is played at discos alongside gangsta rap and European house. Despite deep-seated traditions of hospitality and of religious tolerance, colonisation over the centuries by successive Portuguese, Omani and European conquerors has done nothing to dent the unique cultural identity of the Swahili people.

Left: A *jahazi* at sunset. The Swahili were, and still are, a seafaring nation.

Left: Women dance around a burning hut during the ancient Swahili festival of *Mwaka Kogwa*, held annually to celebrate the Shirazi, or Persian, new year.
Above: The public veiling of women is one of the most visible manifestations of Islamic culture in Zanzibar.

Left: Friday prayers at a modern-day mosque in Zanzibar Stone Town. Islam came to Zanzibar with the rise of the Swahili civilisation and the arrival of immigrants from the Persian Gulf.
Above: The mosque at Kizimkazi is the oldest on Zanzibar, with Kufic inscriptions carved on the walls that date it to the eleventh century.

Above: Antique Swahili domestic furniture is now in demand to decorate hotels and private houses in Zanzibar. A Swahili corn grinder adorns the terrace at Sultan Palace hotel.
Right: A Swahili charpoy, or string bed, with carved legs, is now in use as a sun lounger.

Above and right: The Swahili Room at Breezes Beach Club. Furniture is simple, fabrics are rich and bright.

Left and above: A simple coffee table is given ornate legs in this modern take on traditional Swahili domestic furnishings.

Above: A Swahili outrigger canoe, filled with plants, adds character to the bar on Chapwani Private Island; and **right:** makes an elegant suspended centrepiece to the dining room at Sultan Palace hotel.

Left: An antique Swahili baby's cradle, with a springy wood frame and canvas sling, is one of a pair that decorates the verandah of Imani Beach Villa in Bububu.
Above: A hammock at the Zanzibar Serena Inn follows the same design.

Above: Bi Kidude restaurant at Emerson and Green hotel is a riot of African fabrics, and named after one of Zanzibar's best-known Taarab artists.
Right: A Swahili wedding chair on display at Mbweni Ruins hotel. Ceramic plates are sunk into the walls in the manner of a Swahili grave.

DETAILS ✸ TEXTILES

A Kiswahili *misemo*, or saying, is printed on every lady's cotton wrap, or *khanga*. She wraps one half around her waist, ties the other over her head, plucks the fabric so the drapes fall just so. Then she's ready to go, sashaying along the village street or through Stone Town's alleyways, her message plain to see - if you can decipher it. It might be saucy: 'The sweetness of sugar cane is in the tip'. Or encouraging: 'Love your enemy'. More often, *khanga* are needed to make rivals in love feel uncomfortable: 'The bee fiercely guards its honey' or 'The way of the liar is short'. A wife might sport a *khanga* that lets her husband realise his infidelities have been rumbled: 'You will exhaust the butcheries, while all the meat tastes the same'. In the small-town, gossipy atmosphere of Zanzibar's Swahili communities, each *misemo* is heavily laden with layers of meaning indecipherable to outsiders.

Khanga have more functional uses too - they come in handy as baby carriers, nightgowns, bath towels and aprons. *Khanga* are tokens of esteem given as gifts from a husband to his wife, a mother-in-law to a daughter, or a visitor to her hostess. The tradition of wearing *khanga* originated with cotton kerchiefs, imported from the mainland in the nineteenth century. Today, any self-respecting Swahili lady will own several hundred *khanga*, suitable for birth, marriage, death and any conceivable situation in between. There is a saying that no woman can ever be satisfied with the number of *khanga* she has.

For Zanzibar's interior designers, the gaudy, cheerful patterns of the *khanga* add a splash of colour to neutral spaces. Other textiles - rich Indian sari silks, *merikani* cotton cloth (named for the American merchants who first brought it here) and appliquéd cushion covers - bring opulent life to restaurants, communal spaces, poolsides and bedrooms. Batik trims weigh down the edges of mosquito nets, gauzy chiffon hangs from four-poster beds and cotton sails line the edges of beachside dining rooms.

Left: The gaudy patterns on a Swahili *khanga* attract the eye, but it's the cheeky *misemo* printed along the bottom that really matters.
Facing page: Jewel-bright colours mass together to form a kaleidoscope at weddings, festival and bullfights, or hang in rainbow rows on market stalls.

Left: Cushion covers sewn from *khanga* form a bright, informal space at Ras Nungwi Beach Hotel.
Above: These appliquéd cushion covers are of a style originally imported from Egypt, but now to be found adorning *baraza* benches, chairs and beds all over Zanzibar.

DETAILS BARAZA

In Zanzibari culture, the *baraza*, or bench, has for centuries been a focal point of community life. Benches run around verandas outside traditional Swahili homes, or flank the heavy doors in more distinctively Arab-style townhouses. The long, narrow streets of Stone Town have *baraza* benches built on each side instead of pavements, while in the villages a palm-leaf shelter, flanked by wooden seats, fulfils the same function.

Baraza evolved as a way for Islamic men to receive and entertain visitors without compromising the privacy of their womenfolk. Coffee and sweetmeats would be served on the *baraza* to anyone who arrived, with only the closest friends or family members being invited into the innermost recesses of the house. The Omani sultans held public meetings, also known as *baraza*, to receive petitioners or give visiting dignitaries a public audience.

Today, *baraza* are still a meeting point for all sections of Zanzibari society. Every urban *baraza* is lined with people gossiping, playing games of *bao* or cards, drinking thick, sweet Arabic coffee, or simply idling away the heat of a long afternoon with a nap on the smooth, warm stone. Draughts boards are scratched in chalk on the stone surfaces, ladies sit comfortably to plait each others' hair, and for traders with no market stalls of their own, *baraza* provide a flat surface on which to pile their tiny pyramids of oranges, tomatoes or mangoes. In the rainy season, when torrents of water, sometimes laced with rubbish, make walking down the streets uncomfortable and even hazardous, the *baraza* provide a useful elevated walkway, and pedestrians jump from one to the next in an attempt to keep their feet dry.

For the designers of Zanzibar's hotels, courtyards or terraces lined with *baraza* and scattered with cushions provide a chance to place comfortable, communal lounge spaces in the midst of more formal surroundings.

Left: Public *baraza* line the streets of Stone Town, and provide a handy elevated walkway in the rainy season.
Facing page:
Top left: A *baraza* bench is ideal for filling awkward corners, such as this bedroom wall in Sultan Palace hotel.
Top right: When it's dry, *baraza* are a comfortable, cool place for study or contemplation.
Bottom left: The sunset throws a pool of warm light onto silk cushions in the gatehouse of Salome's Garden, a private villa just outside Stone Town.
Bottom right: Barazas look out to sea, a romantic sunset resting place at Sultan Palace hotel.

swahili style **45**

Left: The *baraza* area at Breezes Beach Club is a soothing, pink and white space for reading or afternoon tea.
Above: A colourful Tingatinga painting matches the vibrant cushion covers that top the *baraza* in this Sultan Palace hotel bedroom.

DETAILS TINGATINGA

Edward Saidi Tingatinga was born in 1937 to a family of subsistence farmers in southern Tanzania. In 1953 he travelled to Dar-es-Salaam in search of work, and did odd jobs until 1961 when, struck by the speed at which western-style canvases by Zairean artists sold to tourists, he decided to try his hand as a painter. He began by using discarded ceiling boards, dregs of household paint and old paintbrushes, but despite this unpromising beginning quickly discovered a new and unique artistic style. Colourful, crowded canvases depicted fantastic birds and animals, dancing tribespeople, and scenes of village life. His lack of formal training led to a simple, direct and naïve approach to natural subjects, lacking in nuance and detail but bursting with exuberant life.

The pictures sold well and Tingatinga recruited members of his family to copy them. Early Tingatinga paintings show flat, two-dimensional animals painted against a plain background. Each is related to a legend or saying from Tingatinga's Makua tribal culture. Despite this, the painting of Tingatinga is a distinctly urban art form, evolved on the streets of Dar-es-Salaam and conceived not as a means of personal expression, but as a method of earning money. With its cheerful subject matter, Tingatinga art is calculated to appeal to the romantic notions of African life held by tourists.

Edward Tingatinga was shot dead by police in a case of mistaken identity in 1972, but his fellow artists formed a cooperative in his name, and the style he evolved travelled rapidly to Zanzibar and beyond. Tingatinga artists working in Zanzibar produce large, complex paintings depicting, alongside the generic Tingatinga subjects of big game animals and birds, more definitely Zanzibari themes such as fish, monkeys, coconut palms, traditional musical instruments and *bao* games. They work on canvas and also produce 'Tingatinga style' batik prints.

Left: A Tingatinga artist in a Zanzibar studio puts the finishing touches to his canvas.
Right: Tingatinga art typically features stylised natural subjects such as animals and birds, naively rendered.

Above and right: Colourful fish are a popular subject for Tingatinga paintings in Zanzibar's beach hotels.

DETAILS GAMES

Stroll casually round a corner in any village or town in Zanzibar, and you'll be sure to come across two hunched, intent figures seated on a *baraza* bench, grunts of satisfaction or derision accompanied by the click of counters. Sometimes a crowd of spectators will have gathered, pointing and shouting garbled instructions. Look closer and you'll make out the object of all this excitement - a flat wooden board, 32 little round holes, and a lot of brown polished seeds, known as *kete*. This is *bao* - Zanzibar's favourite pastime.

Games of *bao* can go on for hours, even days at a time. Experienced players develop little flourishes, scattering seeds expertly into holes, slapping handfuls down triumphantly at the end of a turn. *Bao* is played all across Africa, Western India and even the Caribbean, but Swahili people are proud of their version - 'king' *bao*. Tournaments are held periodically in Zanzibar and on the coast of the mainland - as in chess, one grand master eventually emerges. The object of the game? To secure as many of your opponent's seeds - or pebbles, or shells, or whatever you happen to be using - as possible. *Bao* masters are said to be able to think strategically five to seven moves ahead, a level comparable with professional chess players. Children learn *bao* as soon as they can count, scratching little holes in the ground in lieu of a board and using stones or chips of wood as counters.

The African love of decorative carving has produced a proliferation of *bao* boards of all different sizes, shapes and forms - the board rests on the back of a mythical beast, grows heads from either end, or is smoothed into the shape of a fish.

African resourcefulness is evident in the other games beloved of Zanzibaris - draught boards are painted onto smooth concrete *baraza*, and the counters are bottle tops - Coke for one side, Safari lager for the other. A piece of plywood is carefully traced with lines for a game of *keram* - halfway between snooker and shove ha'penny. And in the villages, children who've never met Barbie or Action Man fashion sunglasses, model cars and novelty hats out of bamboo stems and coconut palm leaves.

Left: An antique *bao* board and its large round *kete* - polished seeds which function as counters and diced combined.
Right: *A game of boa on a street corner of Stone Town.*

Left: *Bao* games, especially those between experienced players, can last for hours or even days.
Above: Coca Cola bottle tops for one side, Safari lager for the other-a game of draughts on a street corner in Stone Town.

INDIAN STYLE

Give me the writing tablet from India
Ink, pen and dictionary,
So that I may
Sing of praise and love for you...

Swahili Song *c.1900*

The proximity of the vast, teeming subcontinent of India, just a monsoon's gust away from Zanzibar across the ocean, has left an indelible stamp on the islands. The west coast of India, particularly the state of Gujerat - or Cutch, as it is more exotically known - was the home of many of the Indian merchants who from time immemorial sailed across the sea to exchange their cargoes of silk and precious stones for African ivory. The ivory worn by African elephants was softer and more workable than the Indian variety, creating a healthy market for their tusks, taken back to be carved into the heavy bangles and other ornaments beloved of Indian women.

Early Indian traders preferred to make their fortunes and then return, satisfied, to their native land, but as the nineteenth century approached more and more began to stay on. Seyyid Said, the first of the Omani sultans to arrive, encouraged their enterprises, recognising their potential as business partners. Forbidden, as British subjects, to keep or deal in slaves, Indians were forced to look elsewhere for business. Arab culture disdained the counting of money, and aristocratic Arabs considered it demeaning to pay attention to their financial affairs. Many therefore appointed Indian factors to manage their finances, and many more mortgaged their estates and plantations to Indian financiers. A new class of wealthy Indian merchant began to emerge. Indian money was also behind the many successful slave and ivory hunting expeditions sent into the interior of Africa by Arab traders such as the celebrated Tippu Tip.

The dwellings of the Indians in Zanzibar began modestly - a rented shopfront with a four-leafed door which could be drawn back to show the owners' wares, and small living quarters above or behind. But as the riches and confidence of their owners grew, the houses got more ornate, and the wealthiest Indians built their own mansions in the style of the *havelis* of their

Left: A Gujerati teak corner cabinet, hexagonal tiled table and richly coloured sari fabrics are combined with African artefacts in this Indian sitting room.

native Gujerat. Their response to the stifling heat of Stone Town's narrow streets was to build upwards - several storeys upwards - to catch the sea breezes. At the pinnacle of the building perched the tea-house, a raised pavilion, open to the air on all sides and hung with silks. In the hot season the tea-house also provided the coolest place to sleep at night. These days the teahouses rise from among the rooftops of Stone Town like the hulks of ships abandoned at high tide, many sadly out of use and in disrepair, holding ugly plastic watertanks or boarded up with rusting corrugated iron.

Instead of thick walls and small windows, Indians kept cool by the use of wide balconies, open to the air, running around the outside of their houses. Balconies became a status symbol - the larger and more elaborately carved the balcony, the thicker the columns supporting it, and the further it stuck out into the street, the greater the importance of the owner. Balconies were often screened with delicately latticed panels of teak or rosewood, which shaded the space inside from the glare of the sun, creating pleasing patterns of sunlight on the floor, and protecting the ladies of the household from the impudent gaze of outsiders. Balconies were frequently double storeyed, elaborately frilled and painted, and a glance upwards while walking down any of Stone Town's streets today will reveal several jostling for position, still intact or gracefully decaying.

The most ostentatious and ambitious of the Omani sultans, Barghash, while exiled by the British to Bombay, gained a taste for the extravagance of Indian architecture. When he returned to take up his throne and built the ceremonial palace that became known as the House of Wonders, he added three vast balconies, wider than anyone else's and supported by pillars of cast iron. The House of Wonders still stands on the seafront today, and its magnificent balconies are the first thing most people notice when arriving in Zanzibar by sea.

But the apogee of Indian architecture in Zanzibar is unanimously agreed to be the blandly-titled Old Dispensary. This explosion of frilled balconies and fretwork gables stands on the harbourfront just along from the House of Wonders, and was commissioned to celebrate Queen Victoria's golden jubilee by Zanzibar's most prominent Indian, Tharia Topan. Topan was a businessman from the Ismaili Moslem community, who amassed a fortune in the later half of the nineteenth century and became something of a power behind the throne of Sultan Bargash. As British influence in Zanzibar became more and more pervasive, he astutely decided the time was right both for a gesture of munificence and a conspicuous display of loyalty to the Empire. He died before his project was completed, but not before he had received a knighthood. The Old Dispensary, or Jubilee Hospital as it was then known, was bought by the trustees of another Indian businessman, who turned the bottom floor into a dispensary for the poor, but rented out the upper floors for profit.

Left in genteel decay in the later half of the twentieth century, the Old Dispensary was restored to its former magnificence by a team of architects funded by the Aga Khan Trust for Culture, and now serves as the Stone Town Cultural Centre.

The newly prosperous Indians of Zanzibar sent for craftsmen from Bombay to carve the doors and balconies of their mansions. Indian artisans arrived to build furniture from the teak they imported, and silver- and goldsmiths set up shop to create the mountains of jewellery both Arab and Indian ladies craved. Glass lamps, dressing tables inlaid with mother-of-pearl, swatches of brightly coloured silk fabric - all were unloaded at the docks of the harbour or assembled in the tiny, hot workshops of the back streets. Indian workmen were brought by the British to work on the Uganda railway, and when that vast project finally ended, many stayed on in Africa and eventually found their way to Zanzibar to build yet more opulent mansions. Indian woodcarvers influenced the decorative traditions of the Arab and Swahili, adding new motifs such as lotus flowers and rosettes to traditional wave and chain patterns that adorned doors, window frames and furniture. Tharia Thopan's own townhouse, built second in height only to Sultan Barghash's House of Wonders, has been lovingly restored, using many Indian pieces of furniture and fabrics, to become the exclusive Emerson & Green hotel.

After the revolution of 1964, many of the Indian houses in Zanzibar were seized from their former owners. Their balconies are now decaying, hung with washing, and whole buildings have become rather magnificent tenement blocks, occupied by numerous families of rural immigrants.

A few, however, have survived intact, lovingly restored to their former glory and used as hotels or family homes. Their windows are inset with panels of green and red stained glass (the colours of the Ismaili set to which Tharia Topan belonged) that cast squares of colour onto the smooth concrete floors. Hanging baskets still dangle from their balconies, scattered cushions covered in sari silk are strewn across the floors of teahouses, and tiny glass bottles, each holding a few drops of precious perfume oil, line up on rosewood dressing tables. Gujerati swing seats sway gently in front of windows in the stifling heat of the day, and the rich scent of sandalwood wafts up from the bejewelled, brightly-clad Hindu ladies who flit through the streets at twilight.

Left: Delicately carved latticed balconies run around the upper storeys of an Indian townhouse.

Above: Carved Indian darkwood chairs and a Hindu statuette lend an oriental feel to this Stone Town bedroom.
Right: Decadent gold mosquito nets adorn a four-poster bed covered with rich Eastern fabrics.

Above: A partly covered courtyard is converted into a sitting room. The ceiling is open to the sky, blurring the distinction between inside and outside spaces.
Right: The top storey has wooden latticed walls, allowing the sea breeze to blow through and creating an airy space for relaxing in the heat of the afternoon.

Left: Stained glass windows cast patterns of coloured light onto the floor of the lounge in the Tembo House Hotel; and **above:** onto crisp white bedlinen in Shangani Apartment.

Left and above: Magnificently carved bedroom furniture in teak, inlaid with rosewood panels, is the work of the Indian craftsmen who came to Zanzibar in the nineteenth century.

Above: Lacy fretwork carving decorates the eaves of the former Old Dispensary in Stone Town.
Right: The interior of the Stone Town Cultural Centre, the former Old Dispensary restored to its previous glory by the Aga Khan Trust for Culture.

Left and above: The gaily-coloured towers and interior of the Hindu temple on Hurumzi street, Stone Town. Despite being a strongly Islamic community, Zanzibar has a long history of religious tolerance.

indian style

Left and above: The sweeping, grandiose balconies of the House of Wonders owe a debt to the architecture of British India, and **(above)** are the first thing one notices when approaching Stone Town from the sea.

Left: A restored Indian teahouse is now an airy breakfast room with a view over the rooftops of Stone Town.
Above: The familiar contours of Stone Town gain a different perspective when seen from a teahouse four storeys up.

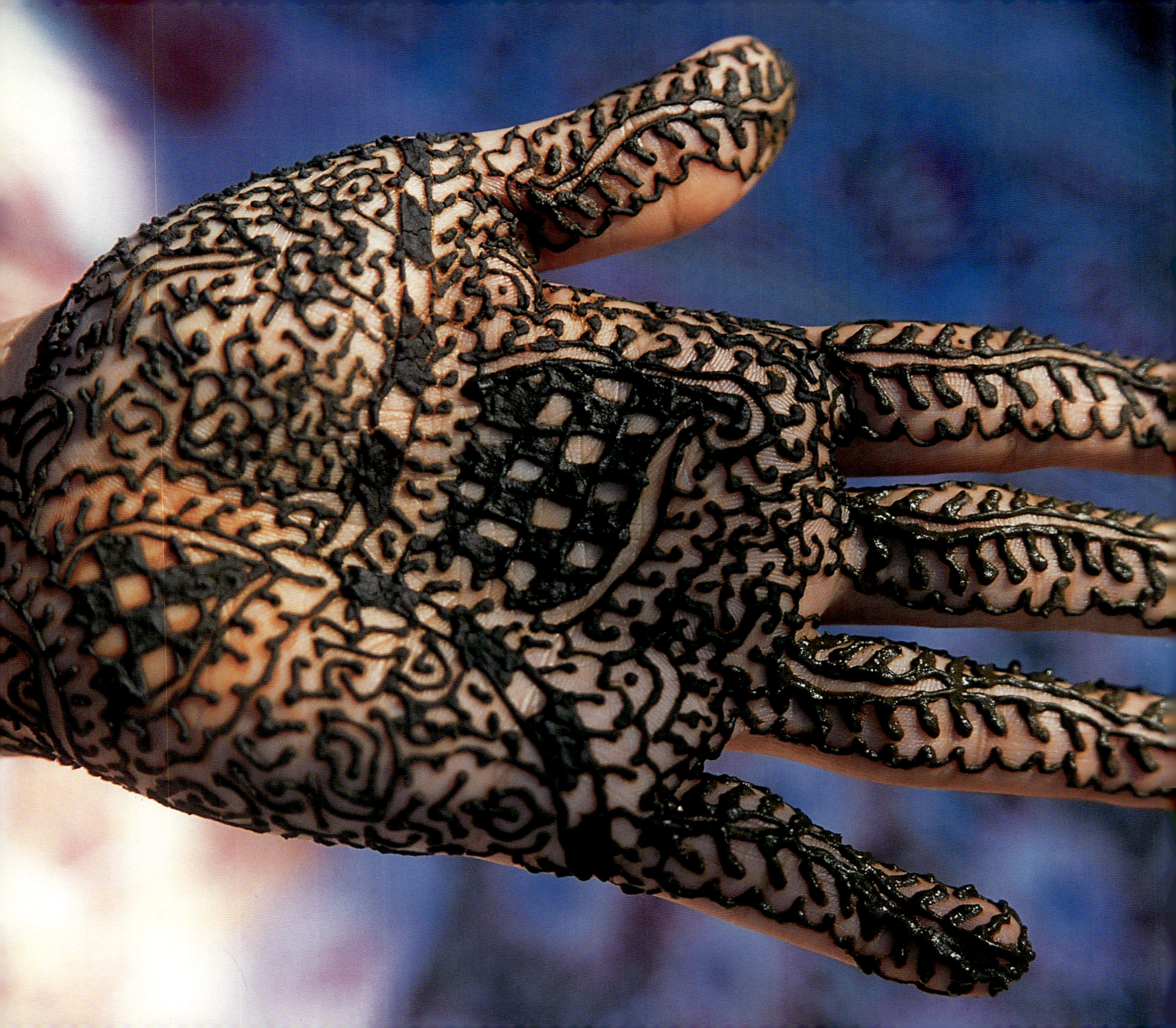

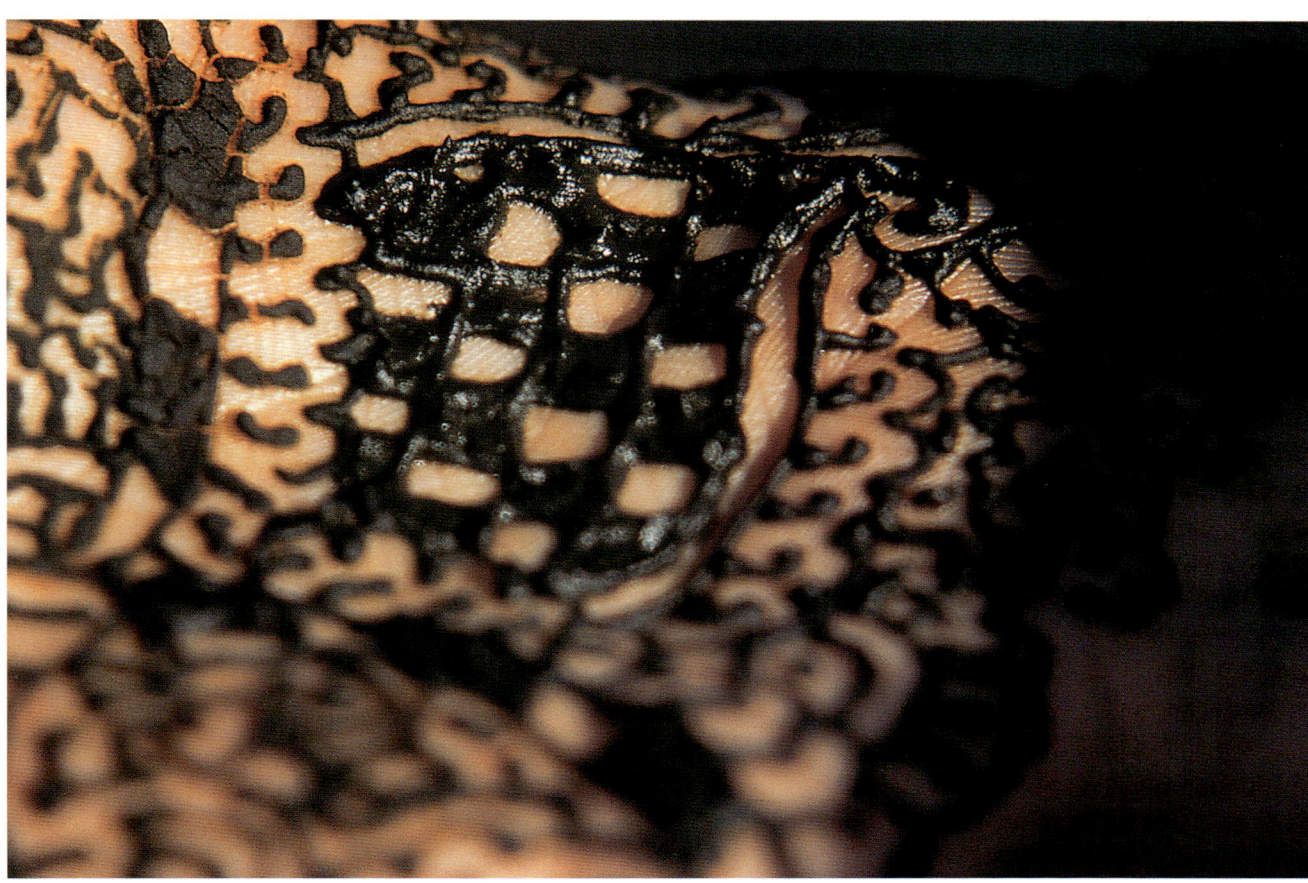

Left and above: Palms are patterned with henna before weddings, festivals or other special occasion. *Mehndi*, or henna painting, is thought to have originated in India as a way of keeping hands and feet cool, and as a method of teaching brides the patience needed for marriage!

SULTANS' STYLE

Their lighted mansions glowed with lamps of brass
And crystal, til night seemed like very day...
...And when they went to rest, they had massage
And fans and gay robed women for their ease
And music-makers, playing and singing songs...

Al-Inkishafi:Catechism of a Soul
*by **Said Abdalla Ali bin Nasir***

In 1828 the flagship of Seyyid Said, ruler of the tiny, rocky kingdom of Oman at the mouth of the Persian Gulf, docked in the harbour of Zanzibar. Since the age of fifteen, when he had ascended the throne after stabbing his cousin to death, Said had built for himself a large and well-equipped navy. Next to the British, he was the most powerful force in the Indian Ocean. His main source of income was slaves. Thousands were shipped every year from East Africa to his capital Muscat to be resold in Persia and the Middle East, and Said collected a head tax on every one. Although Zanzibar was the hub of this commercial empire, the Sultan himself had previously been too busy defending Muscat against his many enemies to visit in person.

Used to the dry, dusty and hostile environment of Oman, Said was delighted by Zanzibar's cool greenery, abundant fresh water and agreeable climate. More importantly, he realised its strategic advantages as a capital - safer and nearer to the interior of Africa, his main source of wealth. In 1840 he moved his court permanently from Oman to Zanzibar. Many of Oman's most influential merchants were already based in Zanzibar, trading ivory, slaves and cotton cloth with American and British ships. When Said moved permanently to Zanzibar, much of Oman's aristocracy followed him. A warlike people, used to defending their homes, they built tall houses with thick, blank walls of white coral, tiny windows and crenellated tops. The only outer decoration was the enormous, brass-studded door, which opened to reveal long galleries running around cool, shady courtyards and tinkling fountains.

Seyyid Said built a large palace for himself at the river mouth in Mtoni, and another on the harbourfront. His numerous wives and children - during his lifetime Said had three legitimate wives, hundreds of *sarari*, or concubines, and 42 children - were divided between the two palaces and his country estates.

Left: Brass pots and tiny cups are used for the elaborate ritual of coffee, served after the evening meal or presented to visitors by their host.

Trade flourished, and Zanzibar became more prosperous than ever before. Said's commercial kingdom stretched further and further into the interior of Africa, until, as the saying went, 'when the flute played in Zanzibar, they danced on the Lakes'.

The best source of information about the magnificent lifestyle of the Sultan's court is Seyyida Salme, one of Said's younger daughters. Most visitors to Zanzibar will come across Princess Salme at some point - her image, a slim, beautiful face dwarfed by a heavy headdress, stares fixedly from a dozen postcards and book covers. Hers was a story straight out of the Arabian Nights, or a Mills & Boon novel - the princess fell in love, from rooftop to balcony across one of Stone Town's narrow streets, with a German businessman named Heinrich Reute. The couple eloped to Germany, but Reute died only three years after their marriage, leaving the 26 year old Salme alone with three small children. Rejected by her family, she never returned permanently to Zanzibar.

In 1886 Salme, now known as Emily Reute, published her autobiography, entitled *Memoirs of an Arabian Princess*. Her descriptions of life in the harem of the Sultan reveal an existence riven with petty rivalries, court intrigues and murderous feuds. But above all it is the elegant simplicity and luxury of her surroundings to which Salme's narrative returns again and again.

She begins with an account of her childhood in the palace of Beit al Mtoni. Placed as it was at the mouth of a river, the palace was full of fountains, water-features and bathhouses. Outside, peacocks and tame gazelles roamed around a vast green courtyard lined with orange trees. The total number of people, including slaves, living at Beit il Mtoni was estimated at over a thousand.

Jewellery was considered indispensable and was worn at all times. On special occasions, such as the birth of a new prince or princess or the purchase of a new wife, the Sultan would open his treasure chambers and distribute gold and jewels to all according to rank. Even tiny children went about decked in heavy ornaments set with precious stones. All the ladies of the harem dressed in the Arab fashion, consisting of a silk or muslin shirt worn over a pair of trousers. Golden bells were suspended from anklets, and the hems of their trousers were richly embroidered with gold brocade. Clothes, heavily perfumed with jasmine, amber and musk, were kept in ornate wooden chests inlaid with gold and full of secret compartments. Arab men never went anywhere without their weapons - silver-inlaid muskets, swords and curved daggers.

The ladies of the harem retired to sleep at night, still wearing all their jewels, in carved rosewood beds, raised high above the floor so that servants could sleep under them. Slaves fanned them all night and massaged them awake in the mornings. Meals were eaten sitting on carpets and mats, the dining table, or *sefra*, being brought in by servants at the start of every meal.

Richard Burton, Victorian explorer and orientalist, described the decoration of a typical Arab house:

'Arabs here, as elsewhere, prefer long narrow rooms, generally much higher than their breadth, open to the sea-breeze, which is the health-giver. The protracted lines of walls and rows of arched and shallow niches, which take the place of tables and consoles, are unbroken save for a few weapons. Pictures and engravings are almost unknown...the result, which in England would be bald and barn-like, here suggests the coolness and pleasing simplicity of an Italian villa. A bright-tinted carpet, a gorgeous, but tasteful Persian rug for the dais, and matting on the lower floor, compose the upholstery of an Arab 'palazzo.'

Despite this tradition of elegance and simplicity, European clocks and furniture were objects of prestige among wealthy Arabs. Among the items still preserved in the Palace Museum are a pair of life-sized portraits depicting the Emperor of Austria and his consort Princess Elizabeth, which were presented to Sultan Barghash, Said's son, in 1888. These were promptly consigned to a storeroom, both because of the Prophet's ban on images of any kind, and because of the immodest depth of the Princess's *décolletage*. Queen Victoria's gift to Seyyid Said of a state coach was scarcely more welcome - delivered in pieces, it was never assembled, because Zanzibar at the time had no roads.

By 1890, British imperialism had put paid to the once-great empire of the Omani Sultanate. By a combination of diplomacy, bribery and the odd judicious naval bombardment, Britain abolished the slave trade in East Africa and ultimately declared Zanzibar a Protectorate. The then Sultan, Ali, became a British vassal, and Britain and Germany between them carved up the Sultan's domains, which had once stretched as far inland as Lake Malawi. Although the sultans remained nominally on the throne, their power was ended and their wealth used up. The last of their line, Jamshud, was ousted in the revolution of 1964 and today lives quietly on the south coast of England.

Princess Salme never remarried, and died in Germany in 1924, aged 80. Cremated with her was a vial of sand from the beach at Mtoni, and on her tombstone are the words: 'Faithful in his innermost heart is he, who loves his homeland like you'.

Right: The interior of the Zanzibar Serena Inn has been meticulously restored and furnished to resemble the home of a wealthy Arab in the nineteenth century.

Above: The interior of the Sultan's Palace in the nineteenth century.
Facing page: The Beit-al-Sahil, bombarded by the British during a succession dispute in 1896, the so-called 'shortest war in history'.

Left: A dhow sails past Sultan Barghash's House of Wonders, so-called because it was the first building in East Africa to have electricity and running water.
Above: The ruins of Maruhubi Palace, built as a bathhouse and pleasure retreat by Sultan Barghash for the ladies of his harem.

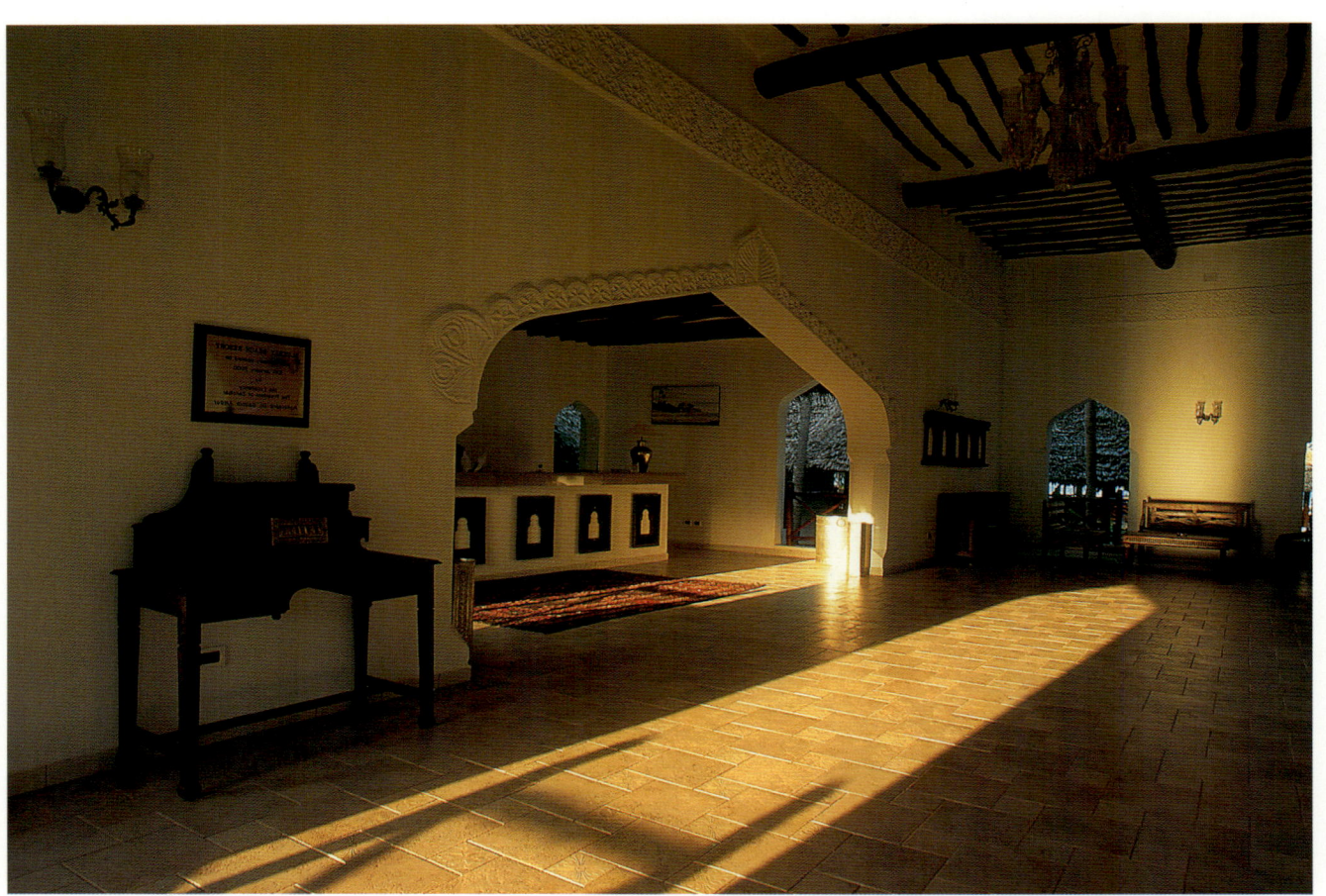

Above and right: The interior of an Arab house is plain, even forbidding, with high white walls and tiny windows. In contrast, the interior courtyard is decorative and serene, with curved arches leading into adjoining rooms and a central fountain lined with mosaic tiles. Here the effect of an Arab central courtyard is recreated in the lobby of Bluebay Beach Resort.

Above and right: European furniture, and in particular English-made wall clocks, became very fashionable among the Arab elite in the heyday of the Sultanate. Many of the original clocks imported from Europe now decorate wall spaces at Zanzibar's hotels, such as Karafuu Beach Hotel (**above**) and Sultan Palace hotel (**right**).

Left and above: Arab families in the days of the Sultans dined at a low table, reclining on cushions and eating from communal plates. The intimate, relaxed atmosphere of an Arab mealtime persists in the restaurants at **left:** Emerson & Green hotel and **above:** Imani Beach Villa.

Left and above: The Zanzibar Serena Inn, once the home of a wealthy Arab, has been restored and furnished with hand-carved teak furniture, thick Persian carpets and crystal chandeliers.

Left: Wall niches, surrounded by decorative plasterwork, fill walls instead of pictures, forbidden by the Prophet. Antiques, fine china or silverware are displayed within.
Above: Whitewashed walls and heavy, carved doors characterise this office building, converted from an Arab townhouse.

Above: A grandly-scaled verandah runs along the south wall of Salome's Garden, a private villa just outside Stone Town, believed to have been the home of Princess Salme.
Right: A bedroom at Salome's Garden, long and narrow in the preferred style of Arab interior spaces.

Above: A raised dais at Salome's Garden would have been the place where lady visitors were received for informal afternoon gatherings.
Right: The crenellated wall of the Palace Museum on the seafront in Stone Town casts a shadow onto the adjoining building. Crenellations, once created for defensive purposes, became a popular decorative tradition.

Left: The entrance to the Sultan Palace hotel recalls a fort in the desert as much as a tropical residence, with a gate large enough to accommodate a horseman or two and high, defensive walls.
Above: Whitewashed, crenellated walls at Mapenzi Beach Club contrast with bright pink bouganvillea.

Facing page: Elaborate baths were a feature of any wealthy Arab household. Sultan Said built baths at Kidichi (**bottom left**) for his Persian wife Scherazade, and Sultan Barghash bestowed public Hammami, or steam baths, for his subjects (**top right**). In Zanzibar today, Emerson and Green hotel is a bath-lover's paradise, featuring deep, round tubs, trailing creepers, mosaic tiles and stained glass window panels.
Above: The interior of the baths at Kizimbani, also built by Sultan Said.

Above: Princess Salme, photographed in her family jewellery after her flight to Germany. Jewellery in great quantities was worn by high-bred ladies from infancy, and never removed while sleeping.
Right: Omani jewellery found in Zanzibar today is typically made from heavy, beaten silver.

Above: The distinctive Arab J-shaped dagger had a handle made from rhinoceros horn and a silver sheath. No Arab gentleman would ever dream of stepping out of doors without his weapons.
Right: A pair of formal *baraza* lead through an arch into the reception area at Sultan Palace hotel, revealing a full-length portrait of Sultan Hamoud bin Mohammed. A dagger is stuck in his sash.

DETAILS ⬤ DOORS

*Watoto wangu wawili kutwa wagombana bali
usiku hulala salama salimini - Mlango*
Swahili riddle
(My two children quarrel all day but sleep
peacefully together at night - the two halves of a door)

The evolution of huge, carved doors as an expression of status and wealth in Zanzibar society began in the Swahili era, but reached its zenith in the nineteenth century, when the buying power of the wealthy Omani Arabs combined with the skill and artistry of Indian carvers. Richard Burton, visiting Zanzibar in 1858, commented: 'The higher the tenement, the bigger the gateway, the heavier the padlock, and the huger the iron studs which nail the door of heavy timber, the greater is the owner's dignity.'

The iron studs, mentioned by Burton and still prominent on the doors of modern Zanzibar, were a throwback to Indian defences against war-elephants. War-elephants may have been unknown in Zanzibar, but the door studs fitted in perfectly with the Arab ideal of a domestic residence that could also serve a defensive purpose. Many doors had smaller windows or doors let into them to allow only one visitor at a time to pass in and out.

Apart from their massive, thick construction, the main feature of Zanzibar doors was the decorative carving that adorned the frame, the central pillars and the semi-circular area above the door. Traditionally, a rope or chain pattern ran around the outermost strip of the door, to enslave evil spirits and keep the family of the house safe from harm. The inner frame and the middle post were carved with abstract motifs such as lotus or rosette patterns, or a decorative theme reflecting the owner's profession - the owner of a fleet of fishing boats, for example, might choose a pattern of scales. In later years the traditional Islamic prohibition of portrayals of living creatures was relaxed, leading to the depictions of lions or eagles found in palaces such as the House of Wonders. A door's carving almost always included pious verses from the Qu'ran, sometimes picked out in gilt.

Left: An elaborately carved door in Stone Town. Traditional Zanzibari doors have carved centre posts, semi-circular or square lintels, and brass studs.
Right: The carving on the doors of the House of Wonders consists of verses from the Koran in Arabic script, picked out in gold.

Above: The lotus pattern popularised by the Indian craftsmen who carved many of Zanzibar's doors.
Right: Brass door studs were another Indian import: their original use was to repel war elephants.

COLONIAL STYLE

...A tea table lavishly spread as only the English can spread them. Round, capacious and white, standing with sturdy legs against the green vines of the garden, a thousand miles of Africa receding from its edge.

Beryl Markham, *West with the Night*

The Portuguese were the first Europeans to 'discover' Zanzibar. In keeping with their conduct in the rest of their so-called empire, they had little interest in the place beyond keeping it out of the hands of their enemies. They built a fort or two, introduced the sport of bullfighting to Pemba and a few choice words into the Swahili language. In fact, the Portuguese words still in use in Kiswahili give a fairly good impression of how they spent their time here: *Meza* - table. *Mvinyo* - wine. *Pesa* - money. In 1698, after 200 years of nominal rule, Portuguese forces were driven out of Zanzibar by the Omani Arabs.

French, Dutch and English tall ships followed the Portuguese around the Cape, stopping to trade in slaves with the Arabs. After the Napoleonic war and the scuffles that followed it, the British emerged on top, the premier seapower in the Indian Ocean. Seyyid Said, Imam of Oman, was careful to secure his own position by expressions of friendship to the British and American merchant ships who arrived in Zanzibar harbour. Treaties were concluded, and the first western consul in Zanzibar, the American businessman Richard Waters, was appointed in 1837. The first British consul, Atkins Hamerton, arrived in 1840.

With the nineteenth century came the Victorian mania for African exploration. The legendary Dr David Livingstone and a string of other explorers made Zanzibar their base for expeditions into the interior of the 'Dark Continent'. Henry Morton Stanley set out from Zanzibar in 1871 on his way to his famous meeting with Livingstone at Ujiji on the shores of Lake Tanganyika. When Livingstone died in Zambia in 1873, his two loyal companions, Susi and Chumah, walked with his preserved body all the way back to Zanzibar, from where it was shipped to England for a funeral at Westminster Abbey.

The powerful Universities Mission in Central Africa, led by Archbishop Edward Steere and one of the most vociferous lobbies for the abolition of the

Left: An antique gramophone, once the prized possession of a colonial official, now gathers dust in a Stone Town curio shop.

slave trade, came to Zanzibar in 1864. When slavery was finally abolished in 1873, Bishop Steere masterminded the building of a vast Anglican cathedral on the site of the old slave market. Sultan Barghash gave his consent to the building, asking only that it should not be built higher than his own House of Wonders.

Today, in the steaming heat of the afternoons, the plaster walls of the cathedral peel limply onto the choir practising 'Jerusalem'. The smell of decay is in the air, but the brass plaque commemorating the British sailors lost at sea and the copper panels behind Bishop Steere's imposing altar - built above the slave whipping post - are polished lovingly every day. Miss Caroline Thackeray, the magnificent spinster behind the Mission's village for freed slaves at Mbweni, donated the mosaic in front of the altar. The crucifix is made from the tree under which David Livingstone, the abolitionists' champion, died in Zambia. Every brick seems filled with the spirit of Victorian crusaders, their whole lives spent in pursuit of a God-given duty to convert 'natives' into useful, productive and Christian subjects of Her Britannic Majesty. And mend the drains while they were about it.

Outside, down an equally crumbling staircase, an unsigned door leads into a musty, claustrophobic cellar lit by a fluorescent light bulb. This was the slave holding chamber, built with shelves for more convienient stacking of human beings. Someone, presumably in an attempt to add historical colour, has left a length of rusty chain next to the entrance. It's sharply and unexpectedly moving.

Richard Burton, explorer, linguist and oriental scholar, stayed at Zanzibar with Captain John Speke while preparing an expedition in search of the source of the Nile. Burton found time to write a two-volume book about Zanzibar, in which he describes in gloomy terms the life of a European on the island: 'What with bad water, and worse liquor, the Briton finds it hard to live at Zanzibar'. This may have had less to do with water or liquor, and more to do with the dictates of European clothing. 'Flannel must always be worn despite the irritability of the ever-perspiring skin: even in the hottest weather the white cotton jackets of British India are discarded for tweeds, and for an American stuff of mixed cotton and wool. Extra warm clothing is considered necessary as long as the mugginess lasts'.

Shangani point in Stone Town became the location of the British consulate - described by Burton as: 'A large solid pile, coloured like a twelfth-cake, and shaped like a claret-chest, which lay on its side, comfortably splashed by the sea'. Shangani was also the site of the English Club at Zanzibar - the first expatriate club in Africa - and the Africa Hotel, established in 1888.

With the advent of the British protectorate in 1890, life grew more tolerable for the Europeans of Zanzibar. The peninsular of Mnanzi Moja, just outside Zanzibar town, was cleared and made into grounds for tennis, polo, croquet and golf. Furniture was shipped from Europe or made on the spot by Indian workmen: long-armed planters' chairs, card tables and writing bureaux.

Windows were kept firmly shut against dangerous land breezes, thought to be the cause of the malaria fever that still carried off dozens of whites every year. Many colonial officials had been posted to upcountry stations on the mainland before arriving at Zanzibar - they brought with them hunting trophies in the form of stuffed antelope heads, crocodile skins, elephant feet or leopardskin rugs.

British novelist Evelyn Waugh visited Zanzibar on several occasions, the first being in the 1930s, and was less than impressed. This may have had something to do with the heat, which he found intolerable and which compelled him to spend most of his time, 'With my head covered in eau-de-cologne, sitting under the electric fan'. When he did venture out for a tour of the island he pronounced: 'Instead of the cultured, rather decadent aristocracy of the Oman Arabs, we have given them a caste of just, soap-loving young men with public-school blazers'. Of Stone Town he concluded: 'In the time of Burton it must have been a city of great beauty and completeness. Now there is not a single Arab in any of the great Arab houses: instead there are counting-houses full of Indian clerks or flats inhabited by cosy British families'.

John Sinclair, the chief British architect in Zanzibar for 27 years, appeared to share Waugh's regret at the passing of the Arab era. His buildings, including the High Court and the Peace Memorial museum, positively oozed orientalism, with Moorish arches, domes, crenellations and cupolas on every side. His style was dominant in Zanzibar during the early twentieth century, and became known as 'Sinclairian Saracenism'. Sinclair's love affair with all things Eastern drew derision from his colleagues - 'The new maternity hospital...assumed the aspect of a Caliph's palace. A cinema near the docks seemed to have affinities with the Alhambra, while the new ariport building seemed to have exchanged nods with the Great Mosque at Cairo'. Visitors to Zanzibar today, surveying the blank, utilitarian blocks built by Chinese and East German architects following the 1964 revolution, might look on Sinclair's efforts more benevolently.

Right: The Zanzibar Hotel, Baghani, photographed in the early 1960s.

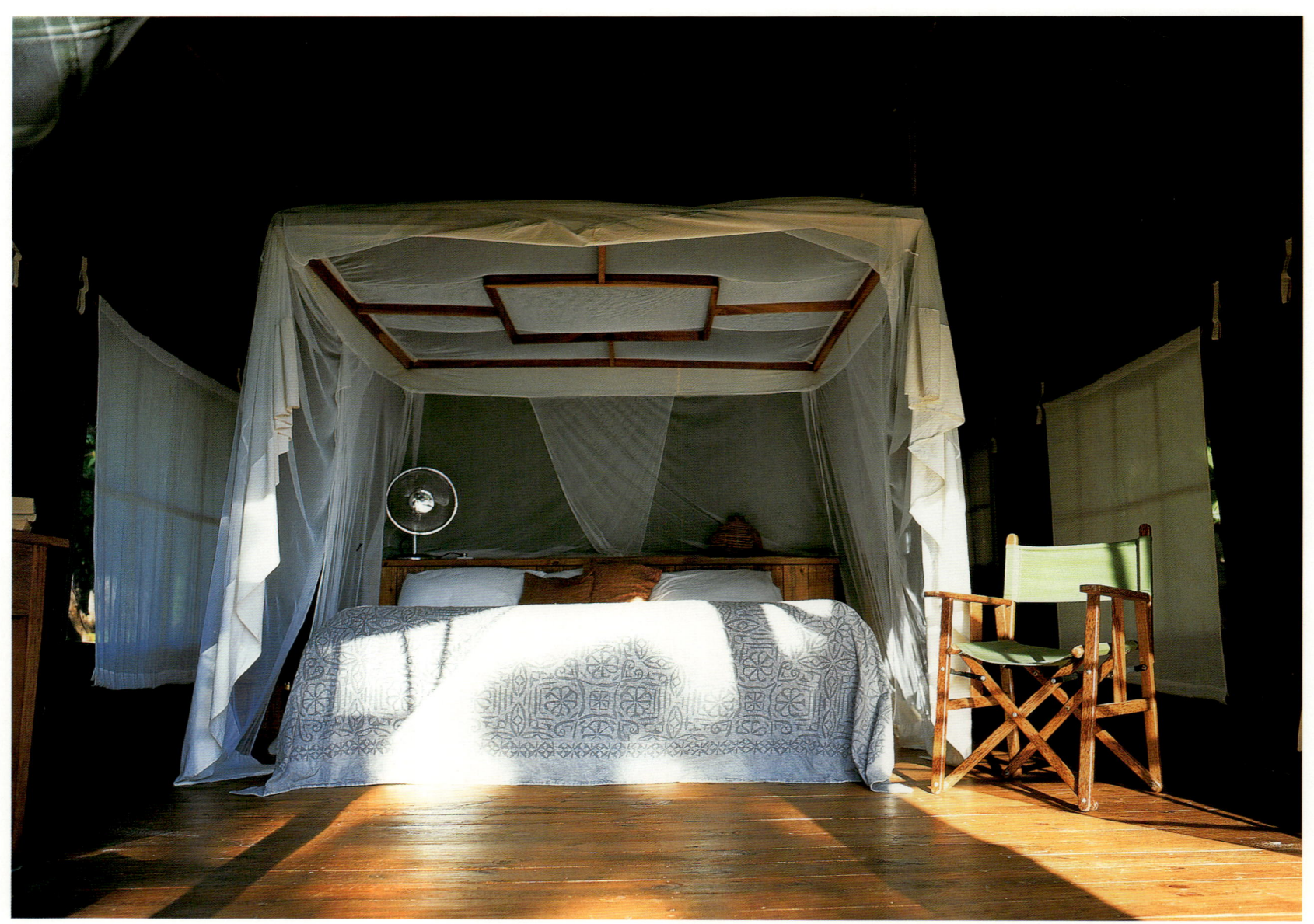

Above and right: The bedrooms at Fundu Lagoon in Pemba, hidden in the tropical jungle that edges the beach, recall the wood-and-canvas elegance of an upcountry safari.

Left and above: Hotel bars, like this one at Breezes Beach Club, have a colonial flavour, with animal print cushions and high-backed chairs for relaxing with a sundowner gin & tonic or post-dinner brandy.

Left and above: Heavy wooden furniture, African artefacts, hunting trophies and cool cotton fabrics characterise this modern colonial apartment overlooking the ocean at Shangani.

Above: The bar of the Zanzibar Serena Inn, which recalls the first-class lounge of an elegant ocean liner.
Right: The lounge of Ras Nungwi hotel is decorated in colonial style, with a writing bureau, straight-backed chairs and sepia photographs on the walls.

Above: Long-armed planters' chairs, an essential feature of any colonial verandah.
Right: Jazz on the gramophone, a relaxing chair and a gin and tonic - the perfect way to relax as the sun goes down - 1930s style.

Above and right: This Singer sewing machine advertising board, written in Swahili, gives a new twist to 50s kitsch and an interesting touch to the landing at a private apartment in Stone Town.

Left: The Anglican cathedral, built on the site of the old slave market in Stone Town.
Above: The Peace Memorial Museum, the best example of 'Sinclairian Saracenism'.

Above: The monument to British sailors on Grave Island. Many died of fever before the age of 25 - others were killed in skirmishes with Arab slavers. 38 perished when the British warship HMS Pegasus was ambushed by the German raider Konigsberg during the First World War.
Right: The bandstand in Forodhani Gardens was once the scene of a reception committee for Princess Margaret. These days it is a shady spot for loungers, a meeting place for friends and a playground for children.

Above and right: Bullfighting is thought to have arrived in Pemba with the Portuguese. In the Pemban version, however, the bull is not killed, but decorated with flowers and paraded around the village after the fight.

colonial style 133

LAND & SEA STYLE

This place, for the goodness of the harbour and watering and plentiful refreshing with fish, and for sending all sorts of fruits of the country, as cows...and oxen and hens, is carefully to be sought for by such of all ships as shall hereafter pass this way.

James Lancaster, captain of the *Edward Bonaventure*, first English ship in Zanzibar, 1592

The spectacular coastline and thickly forested interiors of Zanzibar and Pemba have prompted many lyrical turns of phrase from literary-minded visitors, but are viewed in a more pragmatic way by the islands' inhabitants. The sea provides a living for fishermen, mangrove trees yield poles for building, and spices, correctly prepared, cure a variety of common ailments.

Romantically swaying palm trees, for example, are a source of nourishment - young, green coconuts called *madafu*, sold from baskets on the front of bicycles, are Zanzibar's original fast food. Their husks are also used as important construction materials. The husks of mature coconuts are buried for as long as six months at a time in the damp sand of the beach, being dug up periodically, soaked in salt water and beaten against rocks with stones. At the end of this time they are soft enough to be woven into a coarse rope known as *coir*, which has been used in Zanzibar since time immemorial for stringing *charpoy* beds, binding together poles when building a house, or making rigging for boats. Traditionally, the branches of a coconut palm tree - known as *makuti* - are used in building the roofs of houses. The leaves are shredded while still attached to their central rib, and then dried until they become light and brown in colour. They are tied together in bunches, and arranged along thin roofing poles made of mangrove or mango wood so that they overlap, forming a rainproof cover that can be repaired periodically simply by removing sections. This method ensures the life of a roof can be prolonged after each rainy season, without the disruption of removing the whole roof and starting again.

Green, new *makuti* is extremely pliable and popular for plaiting into baskets or screens to shade an outdoor area from sunlight. On special occasions such as weddings or the Moslem festivals of Idd al Haji or Idd al

---

Left: Ras Kiuyuu beach, Pemba.

Fitr, green *makuti* is fashioned into ceremonial arches, which last only days before turning brown and dry. Palm leaves are also bleached by boiling, then dried and dyed green or purple before being woven into baskets, floor mats and *kawa*, or conical food covers. Coconut wood was rarely used in the past, because its hard texture was difficult to carve using traditional tools. Recently, however, the development of specialised joinery tools has meant that coconut trees at the end of their lifespan can be used as timber for furniture and door frames. Several projects have been set up on Zanzibar aimed at promoting the use of coconut wood and thus reducing the unsustainable felling of other trees, particularly mangrove. Many of Zanzibar's hotels feature chairs, bar stools and other pieces of furniture made from the distinctive light brown, speckled wood of the coconut palm.

Of the thick, indigenous forest that once covered Zanzibar, very little remains today. The interior has been cleared to make way for commercial plantations of spice and fruit, and for the subsistence crops on which much of the population depends. The two remaining areas of natural forest on Zanzibar are Jozani Forest on Unguja island (home to a rare species of Colobus monkey), and Ngezi forest reserve in Pemba. The main rock type on Zanzibar and Pemba, coralline limestone, is known locally as coral rag. It is the usual building material on the islands and is burned in kilns to produce lime.

Although a long way from the dominant position it once occupied in the clove producing world, Zanzibar is still a major exporter of cloves and clove products. Avenues of tall, elegant clove trees can still be seen, especially in Pemba's interior. Zanzibar's climate is so fertile that, in the words of one resident, "If you poke a stick into the ground, you'll have a tree tomorrow". Fruit plantations produce banana, pineapple, papaya, mango, jackfruit and the evil-smelling durian. Spices of all kinds, from cardamom to vanilla and cinnamon, are still grown in large quantities. Frangipani trees and ylang-ylang blossoms scent the air, and bouganvillea cascades over garden walls. 'Spice tours' for tourists are a growth industry on the plantations, with visitors being invited to taste a leaf, bud or fruit and then guess its name.

The breathtaking, chocolate-box perfection of Zanzibar's beaches is a Robinson Crusoe fantasy. The sea is bright turquoise and impossibly clear, and the sand is just the right shade of talcum-powder white, punctuated by rock formations which cast pools of black, cool shade. It's the stuff of a thousand pop videos and holiday brochures. Offshore, turquoise gives way to deep blue as the sea breaks on coral reefs. Flamboyantly coloured and patterned fish potter busily around, nibbling fussily at the coral gardens or grazing in herds, like cows. They have names as outlandish as their appearance - Golden Trumpetfish (long and tubular), Goldsaddle Goatfish (with beard), Bullethead Parrotfish (belligerent and beaked), Picasso Triggerfish (looks like an assortment of other fish joined together) and - lugubriously staring - Bigeye.

The colours and textures of Zanzibar's beach hotels match their surroundings. Lagoon swimming pools are lined with glass mosaics in the exact turquoise of the shallows. Walls are simply unbleached cotton sails the colour of sand, hung from driftwood poles. Bedspreads are blue batik, the colour of the sky. Darkness comes early, and sundowners are a daily ritual, taken on wooden decks overlooking the ocean. Sunsets in Zanzibar, especially on the west coast, are minute-by-minute light shows, with the sun sinking so rapidly below the horizon that it leaves wild streaks of diffused light across the sky long after it has disappeared.

But the picture postcard idyll of an untouched, empty beach exists only in the imaginations of advertising executives. Zanzibar's beaches can almost cause a sensory overload - in the evenings it's hard to decide where to look next as the setting sun illuminates the seaweed beds with a weird orange glow, transparent crabs scuttle out of their holes towards the water and the children run their makeshift cars in circles. Everything happens on the beach. It's a main road, supermarket, bicycle repair shop, barber's salon, crèche and pick-up joint all rolled into one.

In the evenings the small boys of the villages race painstakingly constructed model dhows along the seashore. They're made with infinite care during long afternoons in the shade, perfect in every detail with sails stitched together from old carrier bags and tiny names painted on the side. The tiny craft scoot along the shallows with surprising speed and the boys pound after them, dodging the old women plodding out of the sea with bags of seaweed on their heads. Seaweed here is harvested to be dried and sold - at low tide, all along the horizon is a row of bent backs as the beds are stripped bare within the corral of sticks, like a watery paddock, that reaches far out into the ocean.

Zanzibar's beaches and coral reefs, for years neglected and abused through cyanide and dynamite fishing, are fighting a rearguard action with the creation of designated marine sanctuaries, a programme of education for fishermen, and several environmental tourism initiatives. However beautiful they may look, visitors are asked not to pick up empty shells from the beach (they provide a home for the splendidly furtive hermit crabs), or buy coral, starfish or turtle shells from street vendors and souvenir shops.

Right: A woman soaks coconut husks in seawater to soften them as part of the process of making *coir*.

Left: Sunset at Chake Chake Creek, Pemba.
Above: A boy tenderises octopus with sand on Tondooni beach, Pemba.

Above: Long mangrove poles are traditionally used as ceiling beams in coastal dwellings.
Right: The pier at Sea Club, Kiwengwa beach.

Left: The green leaves of the coconut palm - known as *makuti* - are plaited into screens to keep out the sun.
Above: Coconut husks are filled with plants at Matemwe Bungalows.

Above and right: The colours of the sea off Zanzibar's northern tip are reflected in the blue glass tiles that line the horizon swimming pool at Ras Nungwi Beach Hotel.

Above: The beds at Chumbe Island Coral Park are built on platforms facing the sea. The front wall of the bedroom can be lowered for natural air-conditioning and a view of the sunset.
Right: The breakfast room at Chumbe. The building it stands in was once the lighthouse keeper's house.

Left and above: Seen from the top of the lighthouse, Chumbe's bandas nestle into the rainforest. Each bungalow at Chumbe is a state-of-the-art eco-banda, designed to provide power and water with zero impact on the environment.

Above and facing page: The beauty of Chumbe's simple 'salvage chic' is in the details - a raffia-wrapped bottle for drinking water, candles in jars, a *makuti* basket. or the shape of a crab picked out in mosaics on the warm cement floor.

land & sea style **151**

Left: The makuti palm roof at Mapenzi Beach Club is one of the largest to be found in East Africa. Underneath is one vast space, divided into sitting, dining and bar areas by varying floor levels.
Above: An elevated central platform at Mapenzi is strewn with cusions and popular for afternoon tea. A four poster bed is converted into a confortable sofa.

Above and right: Mnemba, a private island lodge just off the coast of Zanzibar, caters to its guests' Robinson Crusoe fantasies with bedrooms woven from *makuti* palm, billowing cotton mosquito nets and scattered cushions the colour of the white sand outside.

Facing page: From morning iced coffee to afternoon tea, guests at Mnemba are pampered like royalty, with no decisions to make beyond whether to lie in the shade or the sun.
Above: At twilight, tables are laid on the beach for a dinner of fresh fish and seafood, grilled over charcoal and lit by hurricane lamps.

Left and above: Fundu Lagoon is Pemba island's most exclusive hotel, a retreat of utter privacy built along the sweeping curve of a natural bay. Dolphins frequently play in the water around the jetty bar, and the bubbling song of jungle birds wakes guests in the morning.

Left: The jetty bar at Fundu Lagoon is a simple space of wooden decking and green canvas, which highlights the breathtaking beauty of its natural setting overlooking a wild sweep of beach.
Above: Dinner is served in Fundu Lagoon's dining room, surrounded by jungle and fashioned from natural materials such as wood and *makuti* palm thatch.

Above: The reception area at Fundu Lagoon is classically stylish, with tall earthenware pots and unbleached cotton drapes hanging from smooth wooden pillars.
Facing page: Details at Fundu Lagoon are natural and unfussy - a galvanised metal lantern, a coconut bowl for snacks, rough coir rope wrapped around jetty posts, or a child's model *dhow* in a corner of the bar.

Left: The lounge area at Fundu Lagoon is a relaxing communal space, replete with comfortable wicker chairs, *makeke* palm matting, and walls open to the sea breeze.
Above: This dramatic piece of driftwood forms the centrepiece of the reception area.

Above: A *makuti* basket has been given a new function as a set of shelves in this simple, airy beach house in Matemwe.
Right: The sofa is a wood and string charpoy, draped with sea-blue sarongs, and the walls have a gap at the top for natural air-conditioning.

Left and above: Under its tall *makuti* roof, the interior spaces of this bedroom at Matemwe Bungalows in the north of Zanzibar are divided by whitewashed walls of coral rag, allowing air to circulate freely around the raised bed, draped in mosquito nets edged with fabric the colour of the ocean.

DETAILS SPICES

Spice in all its forms does more than lend flavour to Zanzibar's cuisine or provide a handy souvenir for tourists. From serried, triangular piles of bright pink chilli powder, tamarind and saffron on sale at Darajani market to neat, fragrant packets of vanilla beans and cardamom seeds, spices add colour and texture to Zanzibar's everyday environment. Ladies use an infusion of nutmeg as a mild intoxicant to give their eyes an alluring droop, and dried powdered coconut is renowned as an aphrodisiac. The vermilion pods of the lipstick tree, cracked open with a fingernail, provide little girls with a bright red paste to smear across eyes and cheeks in imitation of their elders.

But king of all the spices in Zanzibar is the clove. Clove trees were first introduced to Zanzibar by Arab merchants, keen to break the monopoly on spices enjoyed by the East Indies and the merchants of the Silk Route. The clove tree is a member of the myrtle family, indigenous to Indonesia. Trees are tall and slim in appearance, with shiny leaves and whitish-coloured trunks. In the heyday of clove production in Zanzibar, acres of ground were covered with shady, aromatic avenues of clove trees.

The full potential of cloves was only realised with the coming of Sultan Seyyid Said. He converted most of the plantations in Zanzibar to clove farming by the simple yet effective tactic of declaring that any subject not found growing two clove trees for each coconut palm would have his land confiscated and given to the royal family. Within a couple of decades Zanzibar accounted for three quarters of the world's production of cloves, which were used in hair oil, toothache remedies and perfume products in nineteenth century Europe. Clove smuggling brought the death penalty, and is still a punishable offence in Zanzibar today.

Left: A man works to harvest cloves, detaching the buds of the clove tree and storing them in a *makuti* basket.
Facing page: top left: Spice baskets are a popular souvenir for tourists.
Top right: Cinnamon bark.
Bottom left: White cocoa.
Bottom right: Cloves.

land & sea style **171**

Above: Glass-topped tables filled with dried spices are a popular feature of bars and lounge areas all over Zanzibar.
Right: Cloves drying in the sun.

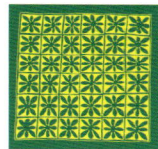 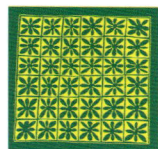

CONTACT ADDRESSES

Bluebay Beach Resort
P.O. Box 3276
Zanzibar
Tel: +255 24 2240240/1/2
Zantel: +255 747 413323/413817
Fax: +255 24 2240245
email: bluebay@twiga.com
www.bluebayhotelzanzibar.com

Breezes Beach Club
P.O. Box 1361
Zanzibar
Tel: +255 741 326595
Fax: +255 741 333151
email: breezes@africaonline.co.tz
www.breezes-zanzibar.com

Chumbe Island Coral Park Ltd (CHICOP)
P.O. Box 3203
Zanzibar
Tel/Fax: +255 24 2231040
Mobile: +255 4747 413582
email: chumbe@zitec.org
www.chumbeisland.com

Chapwani Private Island
P.O. Box 3248
Zanzibar
Tel. +255 24 2233360
email: chapwani@zitec.org

Emerson & Green
P.O. Box 3417
Zanzibar
Tel: +255 24 2230171
Fax: +255 24 2231038
email: emegre@zanzibar.org
www.zanzibar.org/emegre

Fundu Lagoon
P.O. Box 3945
Pemba
Tel: +255 24 2232926
Tel/Fax: +255 24 223 2937
email: fundu@africaonline.co.tz
www.fundulagoon.com

Imani Beach Villa
P.O. Box 3248
Zanzibar
Tel: +255 24 2250050
email: imani@zanlink.com
www.imani.it

Karafuu Hotel
P.O. Box 71
Zanzibar
Tel: +255 741 325157
+255 747 413647
+ 255 747 413648
Fax: +255 741 325670
email: karafuu-hotel@twiga.com
www.karafuuhotel.com

Mapenzi Beach Club
P.O. Box 100
Zanzibar
Tel: +255 741 324985/325985
Fax: +255 741 333739
email: info@planhotelzanzibar.com
www.planhotelzanzibar.com
www.planhotel.com

Matemwe Bungalows
P.O. Box 3275
Zanzibar
Tel: +255 24 2236535
Fax: +255 24 2236536
email: matemwe-znz@zanzinet.com
www.matemwe.com

Mnemba Island
P.O. Box 3107
Zanzibar
Tel: +255 24 2233110
Mobile: +255 741 326575
Fax: +255 24 2233117
email: mnemba@zitec.org
www.ccafrica.com

Mbweni Ruins Hotel
P.O. Box 2542
Zanzibar
Tel: +255 24 2231832/2235478
Fax: +255 24 2230536
email: hotel@mbweni.com
www.mbweni.com

Ras Nungwi Beach Hotel
P.O. Box 1784
Zanzibar
Tel: +255 24 2233767
Fax: +255 24 2233098
email: rasnungwi@zanzibar.net
www.rasnungwi.com

Sea Club
P.O. Box 4095
Zanzibar
Tel: +255 741 326205
Fax: +255 741 325304

Salome's Garden
House of Wonders
Via Manzoni, 6 - 40121
Bologna - Italy
Tel: +39 051 234 974
Fax: +39 051 239 086
email: info@houseofwonders.com

Shangani Apartments
P.O. Box 3417
Zanzibar
Tel: +255 24 2230171
Fax: +255 24 2231038
email: emegre@zanzibar.org
www.zanzibar.org/emegre

Sultan Palace Hotel
Relais & Chateaux
P.O. Box 4074
Zanzibar
Tel: +255 24 2240173
Fax: +255 24 2240188
Mobile: +255 747 415928
email: info@sultanzanzibar.com
www.sultanzanzibar.com

Tembo House Hotel
P.O. Box 3974
Zanzibar
Tel: +255 24 2233005/2232069
Fax: +255 24 2233777
email: tembo@cats-net.com
www.zanzitravels.com/tembo
www.zanzibar.net/tembo

Zanzibar Serena Inn
P.O. Box 4151
Zanzibar
Tel: +255 24 2233587
Fax: +255 24 2233019
Mobile fax: +255 741 333170
email: zserena@zanzinet.com
www.serenahotels.com

Thanks to:

Gerard Schraven of Bluebay Beach Resort, Nathalie Raguz of Breezes Beach Club,

Evano Roveri of Chapwani Private Island, Eleanor Carter of Chumbe Island Coral Park,

Tom Green & Emerson Skeens of Emerson & Green, Gilly Dudgeon of Fundu Lagoon,

Maura Antonietto of Imani Beach Villa, Peter Flueckiger of Mapenzi Beach Club,

Len Horlin of Matemwe Bungalows, Emmanuelle Moneger and Geoff O 'Grady of Mnemba Island,

Graham Wood of Ocean Tours, Tim Hendriks of Ras Nungwi Beach Hotel,

Nicole Poncet Montange of Shangani Apartment, Roberto Merlo of Sultan Palace,

Tasneem Hasham of Zanzibar Serena Inn, Stephen Battle of the Aga Khan Trust for Culture,

Hamadi Hassan Omar and Professor Abdul Sheriff of Zanzibar Achives,

Mehmood and Sean Qureshi of Spectrum Lab in Nairobi,

Frankie Tan in Singapore for scanning and final films,

Mervin and Raymond Mah for printing a high quality book,

and Kay Axmann, Stefan Christian, Emerson Skeens, Keith Hammond, Andrew Smith

and Abid & Bashira Jafferji for allowing us to photograph their homes.

Thanks also to all the stylish, but anonymous people of Zanzibar who feature in the photos in this book.

Special thanks to: